LET'S START
STILLWATER
COARSE
FISHING

Richard Willett

The Crowood Press

First published in 1990 by
The Crowood Press
Ramsbury, Marlborough,
Wiltshire SN8 2HE

British Library Cataloguing in Publication Data

Willett, Richard
  Stillwater coarse fishing.
  1. Great Britain. Still waters. Coarse fish. Angling.
Manuals
I. Title
799.1'1

  ISBN 1–85223–312–5

Typeset by Jahweh Associates, Stroud
Printed in Great Britain by MacLehose & Partners Ltd

Contents

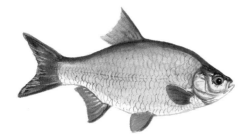

Fish and Location

Many of the species of fish encountered in rivers will also be present in lakes and ponds. Sometimes the species may have arrived naturally in the lake or pond but in many cases man has introduced them to provide sport.

Large lakes can be very daunting places to fish. Confronted with a vast expanse of water, the angler is at a loss where to begin fishing. Wind can whip up large waves on the lakes which then take on the appearance of a miniature sea. Having no real current and no obvious features, locating fish can be very difficult – especially for the beginner.

Lakes and ponds provide a wide range of different environments for fish. Some are shallow and very rich in life while others are deep, rocky and barren. In between these two extremes there is a wealth of fishing to be enjoyed in stillwaters.

Locating fish is not very difficult in a small lake. Shoals of rudd and roach often congregate close to the surface where you can see them splashing about. Tench and carp will grub about on the lake or pond bed, frequently discolouring the water and sending masses of bubbles and bits to the surface. Carp will feed amongst the underwater stems of reed-mace and bulrush where they eat snails' eggs and small nymphs clinging to the stalks. As the large fish force their way amongst the stems of the rushes, they cause the tops of the rushes above the surface to wave about and in some cases to fold over.

When carp are seen feeding amongst rushes like this, a bait presented along the edge of the rush bed will most likely catch them. Gaps in weed beds are also good places to fish for most species. Water-lily beds always look a good place to fish. Carp will venture amongst the lilies, where they feed on snail eggs on the underside of the pads. The stems of water-lilies are tough so, if you do fish for carp or tench near these, make sure your tackle is strong enough.

Bream tend to keep to clear water where they sometimes give away their location by rolling on the surface. When you notice bream rolling it is a safe assumption that they are feeding.

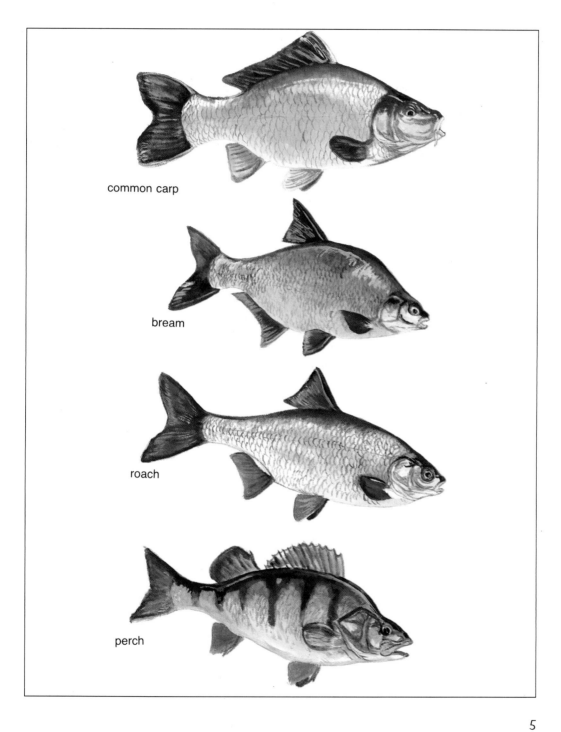

common carp

bream

roach

perch

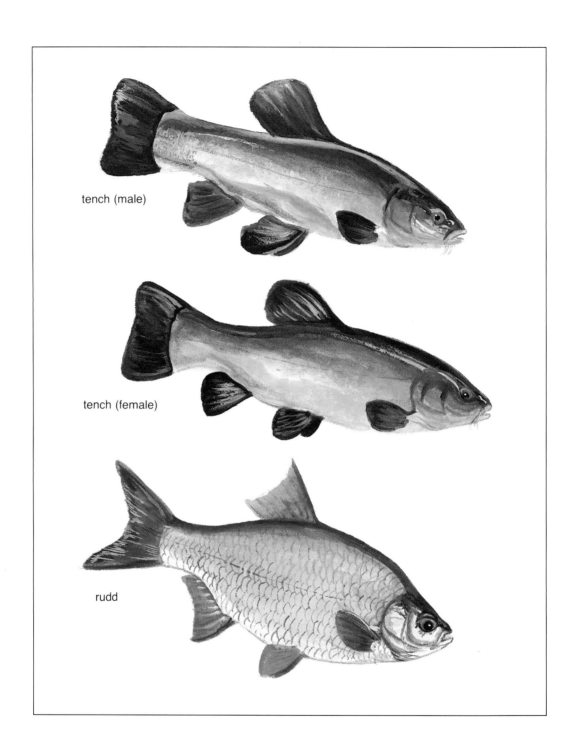

tench (male)

tench (female)

rudd

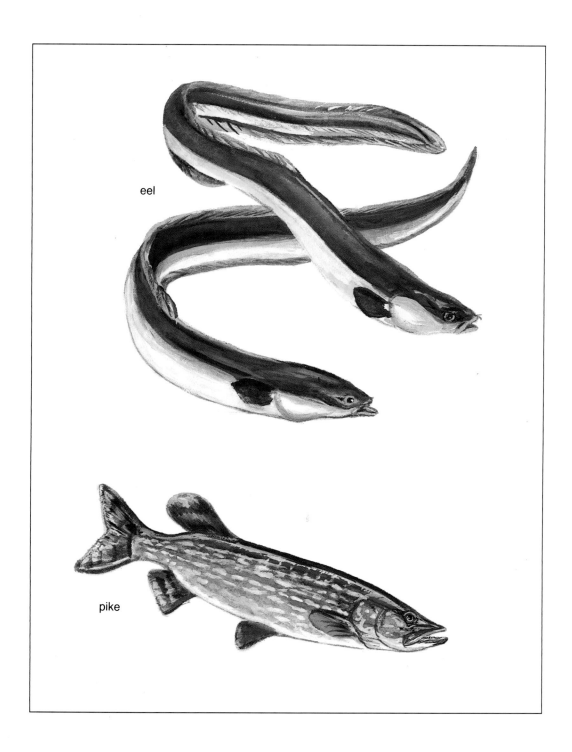

eel

pike

open water

li

lilie:

reeds

roach

reed beds – a good place to locate tench, carp, roach and pike

tench

e, carp and tench

reeds – a place to find
predators such as pike and
perch

reeds

ood cover for all fish

roach

pike

carp

Finding the Depth

If you intend to present your bait on or near to the bottom, the most accurate and positive way to achieve this is by using a plummet.

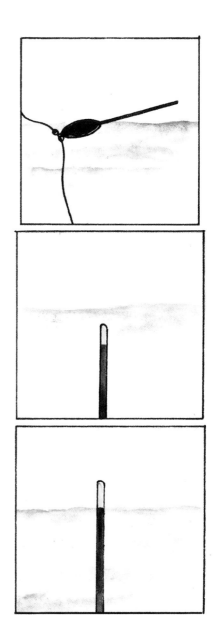

1. Estimate the depth and fix the float in position. Hook the plummet to the end of the line by passing the hook through the eye on the top and inserting the hook point into the cork base at the bottom of the plummet. Then cast to the area that you intend to fish.
2. The float is set too deep. Move the float towards the hook and recast.
3. The float is set too shallow. Move away from the hook and recast.
4. Just right.

The Lift Method

This is a stillwater method ideally suited to fishing for tench and carp. The float is set over depth and a large single shot is pinched on the line just above the hook.

The rod should now be placed in a rod rest and the line tightened up. Now wait – until a bite occurs.

A typical lift bite occurs by the float lying flat on the surface, and then sliding away, underwater and out of sight.

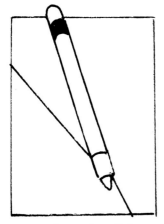

A length of peacock quill fastened bottom-only with a float rubber.

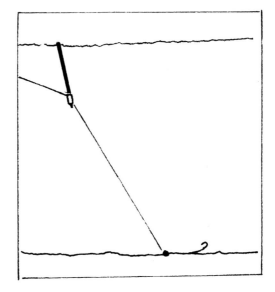

When carp give you this kind of action, you've got it made. A carp hooked on light float tackle.

Float Fishing

METHOD FOR SINKING LINE

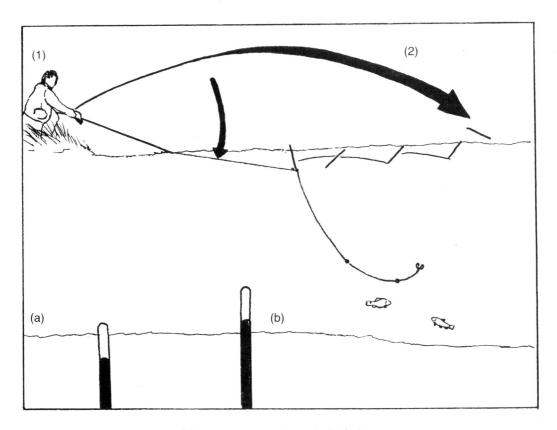

(1) Cast to a point beyond the feeding area.
(2) Draw float back into feeding area.
(a) Position of float when no.6 registers, or if a fish lifts the bait.
(b) Position of float when no.6 does not register (while waiting for a bite).

CLOSE-RANGE WAGGLER FISHING

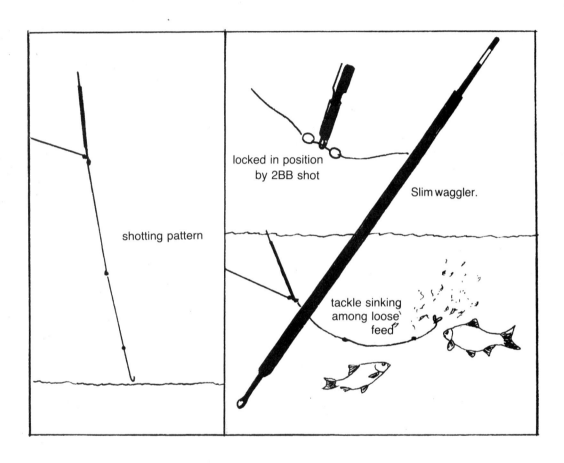

shotting pattern

locked in position
by 2BB shot

Slim waggler.

tackle sinking
among loose
feed

Leger Tactics

Legering is a skilful method of catching fish if used correctly and should not just be used as a last resort after failing to get any bites when using float tactics. There are many situations where legering will not only catch you more fish but bigger ones as well. In fact, it would be true to say that more specimen fish are caught by using leger tactics or variations of leger tactics than by any other method.

There are several important reasons why legering is such an effective method for catching larger species of fish. Most of the larger species feed on or near the lake bed. Tench, bream and, to a large extent, carp are all bottom feeders and this is where it is necessary to present the bait. All these fish will occasionally feed close to the surface and carp will often accept a bait fished near the surface, but for consistent results the bait has to be where the fish feed most of the time, and this is on the bottom.

Legering in lakes poses different problems to those encountered in a river. The most obvious difference is that there is no flow to keep the line taut between rod and leger. Some lakes have a thick layer of weed covering the bottom into which leger tackle will simply disappear. I much prefer to use float tackle for catching fish close to the bank in a lake as it offers the most sensitive way of detecting bites. For fishing at long range for species such as roach and bream, a swing tip is the best way of detecting bites.

Larger species such as carp and tench require somewhat different tactics. A bobbin indicator of some sort will work quite efficiently for tench and, in some cases, for carp. However, when using large paste baits for carp, the resulting runs made by the fish on picking one up require a lot of line to be allowed to run free from the spool.

Alternatively, after casting out, place the rod on two rests and tighten up the line. Open up the bail arm of the reel and draw line down to the ground. Fold a piece of silver paper over the line but do not trap it completely. As the carp picks up the bait and begins to run, the line will draw through the rod rings, flicking the silver paper clear. The line is then free to run from the spool, offering little resistance to the fish. When you decide to strike, lift the rod clear of the rests, close the bail arm and, as the line tightens, drive the hook home.

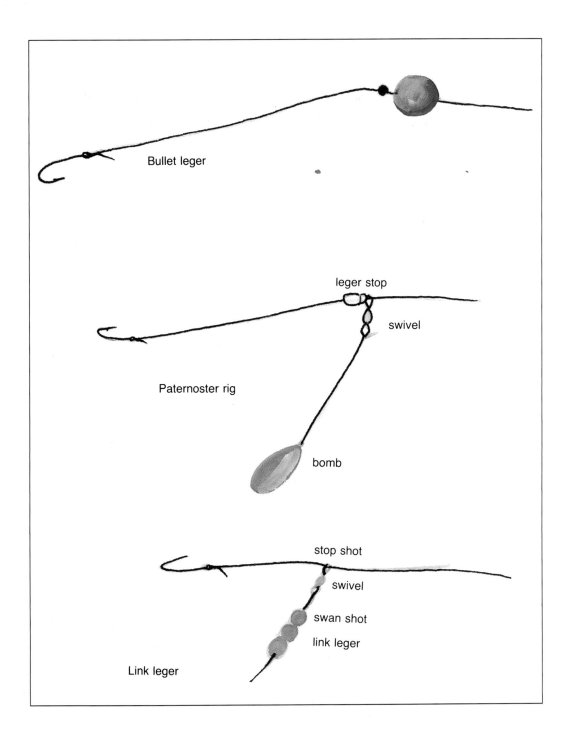

Bullet leger

leger stop

swivel

Paternoster rig

bomb

stop shot

swivel

swan shot

link leger

Link leger

Indicators

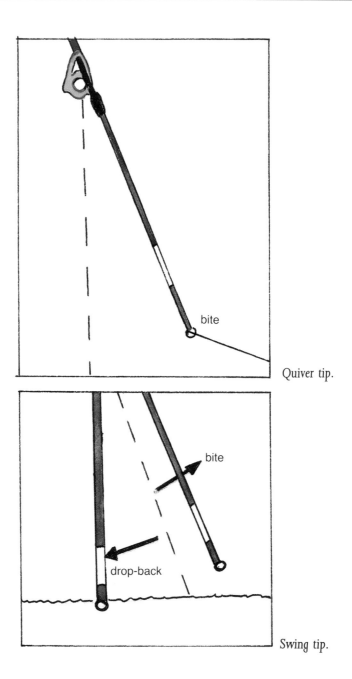

Quiver tip.

Swing tip.

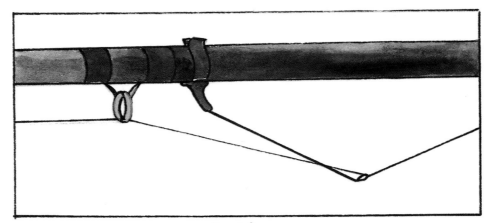

Butt indicator.

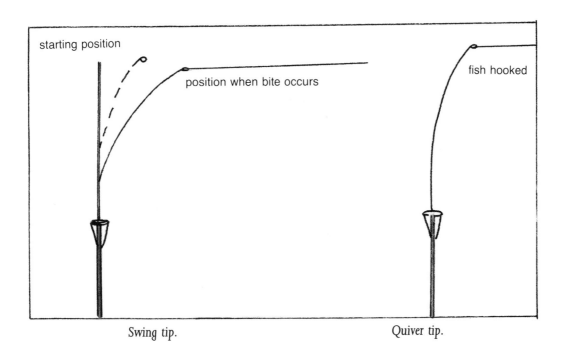

starting position

position when bite occurs

fish hooked

Swing tip.

Quiver tip.

Baits

Anticipation is part of the enjoyment of fishing, and the preparation of baits for a day's fishing greatly enhances this anticipation. Some baits can be bought from your local tackle shop whilst others have to be collected.

Maggot   Without doubt, the most convenient and the most widely used bait is the maggot. More than one type of maggot can be bought commercially. The main one used is the larvae of the blow fly: this is used as hookbait. Pinkies and squatts are small so are used as loose feed. Another type is the gozzer which is a good hookbait for bream. To keep maggots at their best, store them in a cool dry place.

Caster   The next stage of the metamorphosis of the maggot before it turns into a fly. They are ideal as a loose feed bait and are often mixed with groundbait. They are also a good hookbait and will produce better-quality fish.

Lobworm   A very good big-fish bait. Take a torch out on a warm evening and walk out onto the lawn. If the ground is moist you will see them lying on the grass. If you are quite stealthy you should be able to fill a bait box quickly. They are best kept in damp moss.

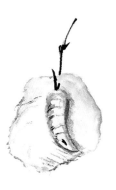  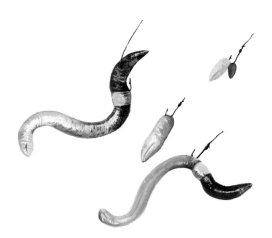

Redworm   A very lively worm. A good bait for perch.

Bread   A loaf of bread can provide three excellent baits for fishing.

Bread crust   A very good bait. It can be used floating on the surface, resting on a submerged weed bed or floating just off the bottom. A bait favoured by many big fish hunters and an excellent carp bait.

Bread paste   Using clean hands, a paste is made by mixing the centre of the loaf with water. Place the mixture in a clean towel and remove any excess moisture. Then knead it until the right consistency is reached. The paste can also be flavoured and coloured during this process. Two good additives are cheese and custard powder.

Bread flake   Fresh bread is best suited for this. Pinch out a piece of bread from the middle of the loaf. Squeeze part of it onto the rear end of the hook shank and leave the bread which covers the bend of the hook in its natural state.

Cheese   A favourite bait with many anglers as there are so many different sorts. A good bait for many coarse fish.

Sweetcorn   A very good bait for carp, tench and roach. An expensive bait but well worth using.

Luncheon meat A great bait for carp and tench, either float fished or on leger. Please open the tin at home and leave it there, not on the bank side.

Potato Tinned potatoes are a good choice to start with. A very good carp bait.

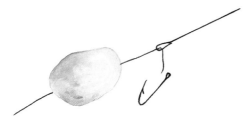

Hempseed On a water which is regularly fished with hemp, this is a deadly bait from the start. It is also a very good bait to use as loose feed or mixed in your groundbait. The seed has to be cooked until it splits before it can be used. Ready-cooked hemp can now be bought and this is just as good.

Tares Larger than hemp and needs a little more cooking. It makes a deadly combination when used in conjunction with hemp and has caused the downfall of many a big roach.

Groundbait A mixture to introduce into the swim you are fishing, or into a swim days before you fish it (this is called 'pre-baiting'). Tench respond well to this. Brown breadcrumbs make a good base, mixed with water. It should have the consistency which allows it to be shaped into balls the size of golf balls. It should not crumble. Samples of baits can be added to the groundbait base – maggots, casters, hemp or sweetcorn, for example.

These balls are introduced by hand or with the aid of a catapult into the swim, where they disintegrate. Heavy groundbaiting can often do more harm than good. Little and often is a more sensible policy.

Knots

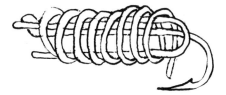

Three-turn Loop knot.

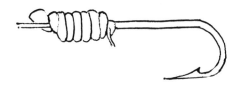

Spade End knot.

Method of joining hook length to reel line.

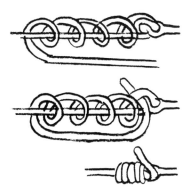

Clinch knot.

Playing and Landing

On hooking a fish, especially a large one, keep the tip of the rod well up and maintain a steady pressure. Never point the rod at the fish. The clutch on the reel must be adjusted prior to fishing so that it yields line when the pressure on it is just below the line's breaking strain.

If a hooked fish makes for an area where underwater snags exist, it can be turned by applying side-strain.

Have the net close at hand. When the fish shows signs of tiring, slip the net into the water and keep it stationary. Never jab at the fish in an attempt to scoop it out. Bring the fish over the awaiting net, not the net to the fish.

Handling and Hook Removal

Always make sure your hands are wet before handling fish. Grip the fish firmly but gently just behind the gill covers. In the case of pike, the jaw will automatically open – don't use gags.

If the hook is lightly embedded near the front of the mouth, it is possible to remove it with the fingertips; otherwise, use a disgorger.

With larger fish, it is best to leave them lying in the damp net while you remove the hook. Artery forceps are best for this. When they are locked, a really good grip is maintained on the hook, which can be gently eased out. A damp towel positioned between the hand and the fish is advisable, as large fish like carp are very strong and need some holding if they suddenly decide to leap about.

Retaining and Returning Fish

Fish should be retained only in a large knotless keepnet, which is well covered by water, preferably in a shaded area. Never keep them for any length of time; in fact, there is no point in retaining them at all unless they are to be

weighed or photographed at the end of your fishing session. Larger fish like tench, carp and pike are best retained in keepsacks where they will lie quietly.

Never throw a fish into a net, but place it in gently, using wet hands.

When returning fish, gently gather up the net until the area occupied by the fish is reached; place the mouth of the net underwater and allow the fish to swim off.

A large fish should be held underwater in an upright position with both hands until it swims away.

Index